Sauces, Candies, & Desserts

A Beginner's Guide

James Shipley

Copyright © 2012 James Shipley

All rights reserved.

ISBN-10: 1480108790

ISBN-13: 978-1480108790

DEDICATION

This book is dedicated to my grandmother,
Genevieve Raschick,
who shared her love of cooking with me when I was a child.

CONTENTS

    Acknowledgments

1   Introduction

2   Equipment & Safety

3   Common Formulas

4   Wet vs. Dry

5   Master Formula for Sauce & Candy

6   Variations for Sauces & Candies

7   Desserts

8   About the Author

ACKNOWLEDGMENTS

I would like to acknowledge the incredible work that my editor, Lisa Vaughn, has done for this book.
Her eye for details and probing questions have made this work far better than I could have managed on my own.

1 INTRODUCTION

Welcome to **Caramel: Sauces, Candies, & Desserts**!

I've always loved desserts. As a chef, desserts are enjoyable to create because people want desserts when they are celebrating. I enjoy making special desserts such as carrot cakes or double-dark-chocolate cakes for my loved ones and customers. I remember that once during a dinner service, I was plating desserts and drizzling plates with the caramel sauce we had purchased. The purchased caramel sauce was not amazing, and I had thought, "I can do this better. How hard can it be?"

That simple question led me to a quick search online that revealed that there are as many caramel variations as there are snowflakes in Minnesota in January. Thus, I began a lengthy journey into the world of caramel and exploration of how to use it for the desserts that I enjoy creating.

The results are offered here as a clear, concise set of recipes, which yield consistently great caramel , no matter what a person's level of expertise is in the kitchen. To be fair, I examined several disparate means of caramel production so that I can explain the utility of each and why I did or did not chose certain options for the master caramel section.

Additionally, I carefully crafted a discussion of safety precautions for the production of caramel, which should be adhered to by anyone producing caramel, not just beginners.

Finally, from my master caramel recipe, I detailed a number of the endless variations of formulas possible in the sections on sauces, candies, and desserts.

If you believe that I have slighted a particular method that you prefer, then you have my apologies. In my defense, I wanted to create a beginner's guide with a method that was appropriate for a beginner and yet would offer the most control over each element in the formula, to allow for creative "tinkering". I hope you enjoy the result.

Chef James Shipley

2 EQUIPMENT & SAFETY

Safety

Safety is the most vital element when creating caramel.

Safety will be a major theme in this book. Don't be dismayed at this, as you'll still have a lot of fun and enjoy your results all the more.

It is important to recognize that if mishandled, then caramel can be very dangerous. In professional kitchens, it is often referred to as

"liquid napalm".

Caramel has this ominous nickname because it burns very hot, often over 300 F/ 148.9 C, and it is very sticky. Once you get hot caramel on your skin, it will be very hard to remove and will burn you badly.

Here is how to take precautions against this burn hazard:

First, always have a large bowl of ice water nearby. Should you get any caramel on you, immediately plunge the afflicted area into the icy cold water. <u>Never let your head and face get anywhere near the caramel pan</u>, especially when you add the cream. Stand as far back as you can to stay safe.

Second, wear an apron and gloves during caramel production (oven mitts are great). This will give added layers of protection against direct skin contact.

Third, make sure you always use either my recommended pot size or one that is larger. When you first start making caramel, it is often assumed that using a smaller pot is fine, as after all, there really isn't that much sugar in there! However, after adding cream, the volume of the mixture will increase dramatically. The pot size that I recommend is a minimum, so if you decrease the size of put used, then you are very likely to have a kitchen fire and to have bubbling, hot caramel cover your stovetop, counter, cupboards, walls, and floor.

Fourth, have everything ready when you begin. Once you start the process of making caramel, it is important to stay with it. This is no time to take a quick phone call or visit the bathroom! A single minute spent away from cooking caramel can mean the difference between perfection and a horrible, burned mess!

Equipment

Equipment for the aspiring Caramel maker is...

Candy thermometer: This is the big one. Make sure that it is very clean and is calibrated before each use. To check its calibration accuracy, place the thermometer in a pot of boiling water. The water should be at a steady boil, and the tip of the candy thermometer should not touch the bottom of the pan. Wait for three minutes, then check the reading and make sure to read the temperature straight on (don't look down or up at the thermometer). It should read 212 F/ 100 C. If there is a difference from this compared to the temperature showing on the candy thermometer, then you can use the thermometer, as long as you make sure you take this difference into account when making caramel and adjust the your desired temperature by the number of calibrated degrees over or under.

Heat-safe spatula: Avoid wood spatulas, as these may have particles that will contaminate your caramel and can cause crystallization. The sugar for caramel is working at around 350 F/176.6 C, so make sure your spatula is rated for at least this amount of heat.

Heavy-bottom pot (non-stick is great) of sufficient size: The pot size recommended in the formulas is a **minimum,** as one smaller could result in caramel covering kitchen surfaces and in fire. A heavy-bottom pot offers more even heat and less of a chance of burn spots in your caramel.

A heat-resistant whisk: You will be whisking caramel at very high temperatures, so make sure that this is rated as resistant to 350 F/ 176.6 C heat, just like the spatula.

Wrapping wax paper for candies: These papers are available online and in baking/confectionary stores. These papers are indispensable for wrapping your handmade caramels. You just wrap your candy by placing it in the middle of the square, folding paper from the top and the bottom edges, and twisting the ends to seal. Note: these papers do not provide an airtight seal, so wrapped caramel candies should be stored in a sealed container and in the refrigerator or freezer.

3 COMMON FORMULAS

There are different methods used for liquid caramel production, and the most common methods all result in making Dulce de Leche which means "candy [made] of milk". Common Dulce de Leche formulas are given here as valuable tools for liquid caramel crafters for some specific interests, however these are not my master caramel formulas, as those are detailed in Chapter 5 and are useful for any application, form, and variety of flavor.

In fact, there are many regional recipes that practically demand that a liquid caramel be made in a common Dulce de Leche manner represented in the next few pages. For many people from those particular regions, this is the remembered caramel of their youth.

The Dulce de Leche formulas are not included in my sauces and candies because these are not derived from the master caramel recipe and do not meet the requirements of flexibility for all desired options.

On the topic of Dulce de Leche liquid caramel, I have three formulas: **Shortcut, Handmade, and Hybrid.**

Shortcut Method for Dulce de Leche:

The shortcut method for Dulce de Leche has three formula styles mentioned in most research, yet the only one acceptable for safety involves baking the sweetened condensed milk in a pan that is in a water-bath. Why?...

One unsafe shortcut involves immersing a sealed can of sweetened condensed milk in boiling water for about 3.5 hours. The sealed can lead to an explosion should the water level drop below the top of the can and expose the can lid to the air. The dissipation of water from boiling 3.5 hours is significant, and 3.5 hours is a long time to diligently watch water boil without a distraction. Unless you can submerge the small can in a very large pot that is full of water and closely watch it, please don't use this method. It isn't safe.

Another unsafe shortcut involves opening a can of sweetened condensed milk then cooking can and all in a water-bath. Cooking an opened can is safer than a sealed can; however, the cans are still not designed to be cooked in.

The preferred shortcut style is safest and involves pouring the milk out of the can and into an appropriate container then baking that pan in a water-bath.

Shortcut Dulce de Leche Formula:

Ingredients:
1 can sweetened condensed milk

Oven:
Preheat to 425 F / 218 C
Place the oven rack in middle position

Directions:
Pour the contents of 1 can sweetened condensed milk into a 9-inch glass pie plate or equivalently-sized glass container. Cover tightly with foil.

Set this smaller glass container containing the sweetened condensed milk inside of a larger container, such as a roasting pan or casserole dish, then add enough hot tap water to the bigger pan to cover at least halfway up the sides of the smaller pan. This two-pan set up is known as a "water-bath".

Place the two-pan set up in middle of the oven rack and bake for 45 minutes. Check the water level and add more, if necessary.

Then, continue to bake for approximately another 45 minutes or until milk is thick and brown. Remove the inner pan from the water-bath pan and set out to cool on a wire rack, uncovered.

Varying your cooking times will affect the color and taste of your caramel. For a rich tasting caramel make sure that it achieves a nice dark amber color.

Properly stored in a sealed container and refrigerated, shortcut method Dulce de Leche will last a month in the refrigerator.

Pros: This method is very simple and provides usable caramel for many different applications. Several ethnic desserts call for this formulation of caramel, and it makes a quick caramel dip for apple slices.

Cons: The procedure is severely limited by the inability to alter ratios in the caramel. It is ineffective in applications requiring either a very thin or thick consistency of caramel. It also does not have the clean finishing flavor that my master caramel recipe delivers.

Hand-made Method for Dulce de Leche:

Dulce de Leche that is made from scratch? Yes, it happens, and in great restaurants, it happens often. The sweetened condensed milk shortcut formulation is extremely simple and consistent, but for real traditionalists, Dulce de Leche can be made from scratch.

Hand-made Dulce de Leche Formula:

Ingredients:
4 cups whole milk
3/4 cup white sugar
2 Tbsp light corn syrup
1/2 tsp baking soda
1/8 tsp Kosher salt
1 tsp vanilla extract

Directions:
In an 8 (or larger) quart pot, on the stovetop, set the burner to medium heat. In the pot, combine milk, sugar, corn syrup, baking soda, and salt. Bring to a low simmer and maintain that low simmer. It will be necessary to monitor the process to prevent the mixture from boiling over.

In the event that the mixture begins to foam up, quickly remove the pot from all heat and stir the mixture with a heat-safe spatula until the foaming subsides. Once under control, reduce the heat and return the pot to the burner.

Stir the Dulce de Leche mixture frequently to prevent caking on the sides and bottom of the pot. The mixture will begin to thicken and change to a caramel color in 30-60 minutes. Stir until caramel mixture is at the color you prefer. If using a thermometer to gauge doneness, aim for around 345 F / 173.8 C for a nice dark caramel, but do not exceed 350 F / 176.6 C.

Pour the hand-made Dulce de Leche caramel into a large bowl to stop the cooking process then add vanilla extract and stir with a heat-safe spatula. Allow the mixture to cool to room temperature before covering or refrigerating. Properly stored in a sealed container and refrigerated, hand-made Dulce de Leche will last a month in the refrigerator.

Hybrid Method for Dulce de Leche to produce candy:

This hybrid method is a common formula that produces a consistency that will make candy, rather than the dip and sauce consistency produced from the previous shortcut and handmade Dulce de Leche methods. The master formula offered later in Chapter 5 will include many variations appropriate for all of the sauces and candies in Chapter 6.

Hybrid Dulce de Leche Candy Formula

Ingredients:
butter for coating the glass pan
2 cups heavy cream
1/2 cup sweetened condensed milk
2 cups light corn syrup
1/2 cup water
2 cups granulated white sugar
1 stick salted butter, cut into small cubes and softened

Directions:
Prepare a 9x9 glass pan by gently coating it with butter. Use a paper towel for even distribution.

In a small pot, on low heat, combine the cream and condensed milk. The goal is to get the mixture hot, but not to let it boil. Maintain the hot temperature in this pot while moving on to the next step.

In another pot (**6 quart minimum**), on medium heat, combine the corn syrup, water, and granulated sugar. Cover the pot with a lid and keep covered until sugar is completely liquefied.

Insert a candy thermometer into the liquefied sugar mixture and keep the mixture at a boil to cook until the thermometer reads 345 F / 173.8 C.

Now, to the liquefied sugar mixture, add the softened butter chunks and the hot cream mixture from the small pot. **Be very careful during this step. Pour toward the outer edge of the pot and pour very, very slowly. Keep your head and face away to avoid the steam created during the adding process.** Enormous amounts of steam will be produced, and the combined mixture will bubble violently. Pouring directly over the center of the pot may yield painful burns on your hands and arms! **In general, for safety, this is a step that should never be done by or near a child.**

Continue to cook the caramel, stirring constantly so that the bottom does not scorch. Cook until the thermometer reads 244 F / 117.8 C and the caramel is a beautiful, dark-golden brown.

Remove the caramel from the heat and immediately pour it into the prepared glass pan. Do not scrape candy from the bottom of the saucepan. Allow the candy to sit out on a counter until completely cool.

When you are ready to cut the caramel, place a piece of waxed paper on the counter and use a spatula to begin separating the caramel from the pan by going around the edges gently to loosen the caramel. It should peel away without sticking, so tip the pan toward the counter and allow the caramel to slide out slowly.

Spray a large, sharp knife with nonstick cooking spray. Firmly cut into the caramels, creating 1" squares. Wipe the blade and re-spray as necessary.

Wrap the squares in waxed paper. The caramels will gradually spread and lose their square shape if not wrapped soon after cutting.

Place the wrapped squares in a sealed container, either plastic or glass is best. Plastic bags are great for being able to write the flavor and date for storage. You may store different flavors of caramels in the same container and just use a sticker or string or other such marking system to indicate which is which.

Store the caramels in the refrigerator for 3 weeks, or in the freezer for 2 months. If frozen, then thaw for 4 hours in the refrigerator and then place on the counter to bring to room temperature before serving.

4 Wet vs. Dry

There are two basic ways to begin the caramelization process. The first is put the sugar into a pan without adding any liquids and turn on the heat. This is known as the dry method. It is often perceived as being an advanced method of production as it requires greater attentiveness to the process of caramelization. Having a thick-bottomed pot and even heat are the two keys to this method. Hot spots are a risk because those may cause some areas to burn before the rest of the sugar is caramelized.

The wet method involves adding water to the sugar until it reaches the consistency of sand, then heating it, slowly dissipating the water as the sugar begins to caramelize. It yields a more consistent caramelization, with a reduced risk of spot burning. This method is significantly safer for an untrained cook and suffers no ill effect for the extra precaution. You must still be careful to not burn the caramel or yourself and must be attentive to the process to avoid explosion and fire.

All caramel recipes, including my master formulas, in this book use the wet method of caramelization.

5 MASTER FORMULA FOR SAUCE & CANDY

Master Caramel

Ingredients:
butter for pan coating process
2 cups white granulated sugar
1 Tbsp light corn syrup
10 oz heavy whipping cream
1 Tbsp vanilla extract
1 Tbsp fresh lemon juice
1/4 tsp Kosher salt
2 Tbsp unsalted butter

STEP 1:

Prepare a 9x9 glass pan by gently coating it with butter. Use a paper towel for even distribution.

STEP 2:

On the stovetop, using low heat, in a small pan, heat the cream. The goal is to get the cream hot but not boiling. If you are using fresh vanilla beans, then add those to the cream to steep. If not using fresh beans or other flavors that require steeping, then this cream heating process may be completed in the microwave, by microwaving the cream in a microwave-safe bowl for about 1 minutes and 30 seconds. The cream should be kept hot until it is used in Step 5.

STEP 3:

On the stovetop, using medium heat, in a 3 quart pot (**MINIMUM size**), put in 2 cups of sugar, add 1/2 cup of cool tap water (or filtered pitcher water), and add 1 Tbsp light corn syrup. Cover the pot with a lid, bring to a boil, and leave covered for 5 minutes while boiling. This will allow the sugar to liquefy, and the steam produced from boiling will wash any rogue sugar crystals off the sides of the pot and back into the liquid. After the sugar has liquefied and has boiled for 5 minutes, remove the lid from the sugar. **Do not stir. Leave the heat on medium.**

STEP 4:

Continuously observe the sugar mixture in pot, as the transition from clear liquid to rich amber color is very rapid. It is important to remain vigilant during this process. As the sugar begins to take on an amber hue, you have entered your caramel window of opportunity. For a deep, rich caramel flavor you want the caramel to come as close to the edge as possible but not to begin burning. In terms of temperature, this edge lies exactly at 349 F/ 176.1 C. At 350 F/ 176.6 C caramel burns. Once it burns, throw it away and start over, as there is no hope to recover or use burned caramel.

I don't recommend using a thermometer for this part of the process. Use your nose and eyes. If you are making a variation that specifically uses brown sugar, then use your thermometer! After a few batches you will learn how to spot the shade of amber that means great caramel to you. You may like it slightly lighter in some cases, especially if you are infusing the caramel with other flavors.

STEP 5:

Once the caramel is at the proper color, remove the pot from the burner, add the butter, and whisk until combined. Then, carefully add the heated cream, vanilla, lemon juice, and salt. **Be very careful during this step. Pour toward the outer edge of the pot and pour very, very slowly. Keep your head and face away to avoid the steam created during the adding process.** Enormous amounts of steam will be produced, and the combined mixture will bubble violently. Pouring directly over the center of the pot may yield painful burns on your hands and arms! **In general, for safety, this is a step that should never be done by or near a child.** Whisk the mixture well to combine.

STEP 6 **For Sauce:**

Pour finished caramel sauce into a sealable container and allow to cool, uncovered, on a wire rack, until it is at room temperature. Refrigerate any unused caramel sauce in a sealable, covered container. Will keep for 3 weeks. Sauce may be frozen up to a month; to thaw, place the sealed container in the refrigerator for 4 hours and then place it on a countertop until the sauce comes up to room temperature before being served or used.

If making caramel candies complete STEP 5 and return pot to medium heat. Then…

STEP 6 **For Candy:**

Whisking occasionally, bring temperature to between 235 F/ 112.7C and 244 F/ 117.7C. At 235 F/ 112.7C, the caramel will just barely set at room temperature, will be very soft and melty in your mouth, but will set well in the refrigerator. At 244 F you will have a very firm-set caramel that will be extra chewy. I personally prefer going to 240 F/115.5 C for most caramels, unless you like a really chewy caramel. Find the number that works best for you.

STEP 7

Remove the caramel pot from the heat and immediately pour the caramel into the prepared glass pan. Do not scrape the candy from the bottom of the pot. Allow the candy to sit out in the pan, uncovered, on a wire rack, until completely cool.

STEP 8

When you are ready to cut the caramel into candies, place a piece of waxed paper on the counter and use a spatula to begin separating the caramel from the pan by going around the edges gently to loosen the caramel. It should peel away without sticking, so tip the pan toward the counter and allow the caramel to slide out slowly.

STEP 9

Spray a large, sharp knife with nonstick cooking spray. Firmly cut into the caramels, creating 1" squares. Wipe the blade and re-spray as necessary.

STEP 10

Wrap the squares in waxed paper. The caramels will gradually spread and lose their square shape if not wrapped soon after cutting.

STEP 11

Place the wrapped squares in a sealed container, either plastic or glass is best. Plastic bags are great for being able to write the flavor and date for storage. You may store different flavors of caramels in the same container and just use a sticker or string or other such marking system to indicate which is which.

Store the caramels in the refrigerator for 3 weeks or in the freezer for 2 months. If frozen, then thaw for 4 hours in the refrigerator and then place on the countertop to bring to room temperature before serving or using.

6 VARIATIONS FOR SAUCES & CANDIES

Whiskey Caramel Sauce & Candy

1 Master Formula for Caramel
1/4 cup whiskey or bourbon (quality is important)

Note: When using whiskey, the temperatures for the caramel sauce and candy will not vary from the Master Formula for Caramel original guidelines.

To make Sauce:

Prepare the Master Caramel Formula according to the sauce directions in Chapter 5. After completing all of STEP 5, add the whiskey and stir again to combine. Return to the Master Caramel Formula and complete STEP 6 For Sauce.

To make Candy:

Prepare the Master Caramel Formula according to the candy directions in Chapter 5. After completing all of STEP 5, add the whiskey and stir again to combine, and then return pot to medium heat and Return to the Master Caramel Formula and complete STEP 6 For Candy through STEP 11.

Ginger Caramel Sauce & Candy

1 Master Formula for Caramel
1/3 cup of candied ginger that has been finely minced

Note: When using candied ginger, the temperatures for the caramel sauce and candy will not vary from the Master Formula for Caramel original guidelines. Also, the finer the mince, the better the candied ginger will work for flavor and consistency.

To make Sauce:

Prepare the Master Caramel Formula according to the sauce directions in Chapter 5. In Step 2, use only the stovetop method and add the minced ginger to the heavy cream, then allow to steep for at least 10 minutes. The goal is to get the cream hot but not boiling. The cream should be kept hot until it is used in Step 5. Return to the Master Caramel Formula and complete STEP 3 through STEP 6 For Sauce.

To make Candy:

Prepare the Master Caramel Formula according to the candy directions in Chapter 5. In Step 2, use only the stovetop method and add the minced ginger to the heavy cream, then allow to steep for at least 10 minutes. The goal is to get the cream hot but not boiling. The cream should be kept hot until it is used in Step 5. Return to the Master Caramel Formula and complete STEP 3 through STEP 11, making sure to use STEP 6 For Candy.

Pumpkin Caramel Sauce & Candy

1 Master Formula for Caramel
1/3 cup canned pumpkin puree
1 tsp pumpkin pie spice

Notes: When using canned pumpkin puree, the temperatures for the caramel sauce and candy will not vary from the Master Formula for Caramel original guidelines. Also, spice and puree should be combined before adding to the cream.

To make Sauce:

Prepare the Master Caramel Formula according to the sauce directions in Chapter 5. In Step 2, use only the stovetop method and add the spiced pumpkin puree mixture to the heavy cream, then allow to steep for at least 5 minutes. The goal is to get the cream hot but not boiling. The cream should be kept hot until it is used in Step 5. Return to the Master Caramel Formula and complete STEP 3 through STEP 6 For Sauce.

To make Candy:

Prepare the Master Caramel Formula according to the candy directions in Chapter 5. In Step 2, use only the stovetop method and add the spiced pumpkin puree mixture to the heavy cream, then allow to steep for at least 5 minutes. The goal is to get the cream hot but not boiling. The cream should be kept hot until it is used in Step 5. Return to the Master Caramel Formula and complete STEP 3 through STEP 11, making sure to use STEP 6 For Candy.

Apple Cider Caramel Sauce & Candy

1 Master Formula for Caramel **with the following changes:**
   STEP 2: Add 1/2 tsp cinnamon
   STEP 3: Substitute 2 cups packed light brown sugar instead of the 2 cups of white sugar.
   STEP 3: Substitute wetting the sugar with 1 cup apple cider vinegar instead of the 1/2 cup of tap water
   STEP 4: Since you are making a variation that specifically uses brown sugar, then use your thermometer! Your eyes will be deceived on the caramel color due to the color of the brown sugar, so the thermometer is a key tool now.

Notes: When using these changes, the temperatures for the caramel sauce and candy will not vary from the Master Formula for Caramel original guidelines. The strong vinegar smell during cooking will not be present in the finished caramel.

To make Sauce:

Prepare the Master Caramel Formula according to the sauce directions in Chapter 5. In Step 2, use only the stovetop method and add the cinnamon to the heavy cream, then allow to steep for at least 5 minutes. The goal is to get the cream hot but not boiling. The cream should be kept hot until it is used in Step 5. Return to the Master Caramel Formula and complete STEP 3 (using the STEP 3 substitutions listed above) through STEP 6 For Sauce.

To make Candy:

Prepare the Master Caramel Formula according to the candy directions in Chapter 5. In Step 2, use only the stovetop method and add the spiced pumpkin puree mixture to the heavy cream, then allow to steep for at least 5 minutes. The goal is to get the cream hot but not boiling. The cream should be kept hot until it is used in Step 5. Return to the Master Caramel Formula and complete STEP 3 (using the STEP 3 substitutions listed above) through STEP 11, making sure to use STEP 6 For Candy.

Cinnamon Vanilla Caramel Sauce & Candy

1 Master Formula for Caramel
1 whole vanilla bean, split and seeded (keep the seeds)
1 3-inch stick cinnamon

Note: When using vanilla and cinnamon, the temperatures for the caramel sauce and candy will not vary from the Master Formula for Caramel original guidelines. Also, depending on the variety/source of the vanilla bean, the vanilla flavor will be different, so experiment with different ones to find your favorites.

To make Sauce:

Prepare the Master Caramel Formula according to the sauce directions in Chapter 5. In Step 2, use only the stovetop method and add the vanilla bean, vanilla seeds, and cinnamon to the heavy cream, then allow to steep for at least 10 minutes. The goal is to get the cream hot but not boiling. Strain out the beans and seeds out with a fine mesh strainer. Return the infused cream to the pot to keep hot. The cream should be kept hot until it is used in Step 5. Return to the Master Caramel Formula and complete STEP 3 through STEP 6 For Sauce.

To make Candy:

Prepare the Master Caramel Formula according to the candy directions in Chapter 5. In Step 2, use only the stovetop method and add the vanilla bean, vanilla seeds, and cinnamon to the heavy cream, then allow to steep for at least 10 minutes. The goal is to get the cream hot but not boiling. Strain out the beans and seeds out with a fine mesh strainer. Return the infused cream to the pot to keep hot. The cream should be kept hot until it is used in Step 5. Return to the Master Caramel Formula and complete STEP 3 through STEP 11, making sure to use STEP 6 For Candy.

Chocolate Caramel Sauce

1 Master Formula for Caramel
1/2 cup chocolate chips (dark, milk, white, or special flavor)

Note: When using chocolate chips, the temperatures for the caramel sauce and candy will not vary from the Master Formula for Caramel original guidelines.

To make Sauce:

Prepare the Master Caramel Formula according to the sauce directions in Chapter 5. After completing all of STEP 5, add the chocolate chips and stir again to combine. Return to the Master Caramel Formula and complete STEP 6 For Sauce.

To make Candy:

Prepare the Master Caramel Formula according to the candy directions in Chapter 5, including all of STEP 6 for Candy. At the **beginning of STEP 7**, just after you remove the pot from the heat source, add the chocolate chips, and stir again to combine. Return to the Master Caramel Formula and complete the rest of **STEP 7** through STEP 11.

Chocolate Marshmallow Caramel Sauce & Candy

1 Master Formula for Caramel
1/2 cup chocolate chips (dark, milk, white, or special flavor)
1/2 cup mini marshmallows

Note: When using chocolate chips with marshmallows, the temperatures for the caramel sauce and candy will not vary from the Master Formula for Caramel original guidelines.

To make Sauce:

Prepare the Master Caramel Formula according to the sauce directions in Chapter 5. After completing all of STEP 5, add the chocolate chips and the mini marshmallows and stir again to combine. Return to the Master Caramel Formula and complete STEP 6 For Sauce.

To make Candy:

Prepare the Master Caramel Formula according to the candy directions in Chapter 5, including all of STEP 6 for Candy. At the **beginning of STEP 7**, just after you remove the pot from the heat source, add the chocolate chips and the mini marshmallows, and stir again to combine. Return to the Master Caramel Formula and complete the rest of **STEP 7** through STEP 11.

Almond Caramel Sauce & Candy

For Sauce Only:
1 Master Formula for Caramel
1 Tbsp **almond** extract

For Candy Only:
1 Master Formula for Caramel
1 Tbsp almond extract
1/2 cup slivered almonds

Note: When using almonds and almond extract, the temperatures for the caramel sauce and candy will not vary from the Master Formula for Caramel original guidelines.

To make Sauce:

Prepare the Master Caramel Formula according to the sauce directions in Chapter 5. After completing all of STEP 5, add **only** the almond extract and stir again to combine. Return to the Master Caramel Formula and complete STEP 6 For Sauce. (no almonds are to be used in the sauce, just the extract, as otherwise the sauce would end up lumpy)

To make Candy:

Prepare the Master Caramel Formula according to the candy directions in Chapter 5. After completing all of STEP 5, add the almonds **and** almond extract and stir again to combine, and then return pot to medium heat and Return to the Master Caramel Formula and complete STEP 6 For Candy through STEP 11.

Mayan Chocolate Caramel Sauce & Candy

1 Master Formula for Caramel
1 tsp cinnamon
1/4 tsp cayenne pepper
1/2 cup chocolate chips (dark bittersweet)

Note: When using cinnamon, cayenne pepper, and chocolate chips, the temperatures for the caramel sauce and candy will not vary from the Master Formula for Caramel original guidelines.

To make Sauce:

Prepare the Master Caramel Formula according to the sauce directions in Chapter 5. In Step 2, use only the stovetop method and add the cinnamon and cayenne pepper to the heavy cream, then allow to steep for at least 10 minutes. The goal is to get the cream hot but not boiling. The cream should be kept hot until it is used in Step 5. Return to the Master Caramel Formula and complete STEP 3 through STEP 5.

After completing all of STEP 5, add the chocolate chips and stir again to combine. Return to the Master Caramel Formula and complete STEP 6 For Sauce.

To make Candy:

Prepare the Master Caramel Formula according to the candy directions in Chapter 5. In Step 2, use only the stovetop method and add the cinnamon and cayenne pepper to the heavy cream, then allow to steep for at least 10 minutes. The goal is to get the cream hot but not boiling. The cream should be kept hot until it is used in Step 5.

Return to the Master Caramel Formula and complete STEP 3 through STEP 6 for Candy. At the **beginning of STEP 7**, just after you remove the pot from the heat source, add the chocolate chips, and stir again to combine. Return to the Master Caramel Formula and complete the rest of **STEP 7** through STEP 11.

Chai Caramel Sauce & Candy

1 Master Formula for Caramel
3 Tbsp loose-leaf chai tea

Note: When using chai tea, the temperatures for the caramel sauce and candy will not vary from the Master Formula for Caramel original guidelines. Also, depending on the variety of the chai tea, the chai flavor will be different, so experiment with different ones to find your favor

To make Sauce:

Prepare the Master Caramel Formula according to the sauce directions in Chapter 5. In Step 2, use only the stovetop method and add the chai tea leaves to the heavy cream, then allow to steep for at least 10 minutes. The goal is to get the cream hot but not boiling. Strain the leaves out with a fine mesh strainer. Return the infused cream to the pot to keep hot. The cream should be kept hot until it is used in Step 5. Return to the Master Caramel Formula and complete STEP 3 through STEP 6 For Sauce.

To make Candy:

Prepare the Master Caramel Formula according to the candy directions in Chapter 5. In Step 2, use only the stovetop method and add the chai tea leaves to the heavy cream, then allow to steep for at least 10 minutes. The goal is to get the cream hot but not boiling. Strain the leaves out with a fine mesh strainer. Return the infused cream to the pot to keep hot. The cream should be kept hot until it is used in Step 5. Return to the Master Caramel Formula and complete STEP 3 through STEP 11, making sure to use STEP 6 For Candy.

Raspberry Caramel Sauce & Candy

1 Master Formula for Caramel
1/2 cup seedless raspberry jam

Notes: Make sure you are using the best jam you can find, and seedless is important for maintaining a creamy texture. When using jam, the temperatures for the caramel sauce and candy will not vary from the Master Formula for Caramel original guidelines. Also, depending on the variety of the jam, the raspberry flavor will be different, so experiment with different ones to find your favorites.

To make Sauce:

Prepare the Master Caramel Formula according to the sauce directions in Chapter 5. In Step 2, use only the stovetop method and add the raspberry jam to the heavy cream, stir to combine, then allow to steep for at least 10 minutes. The goal is to get the cream hot but not boiling. The cream should be kept hot until it is used in Step 5. Return to the Master Caramel Formula and complete STEP 3 through STEP 6 For Sauce.

To make Candy:

Prepare the Master Caramel Formula according to the candy directions in Chapter 5. In Step 2, use only the stovetop method and add the raspberry jam to the heavy cream, stir to combine, then allow to steep for at least 10 minutes. The goal is to get the cream hot but not boiling. The cream should be kept hot until it is used in Step 5. Return to the Master Caramel Formula and complete STEP 3 through STEP 11, making sure to use STEP 6 For Candy.

Orange Caramel Sauce & Candy

1 Master Formula for Caramel
1/2 cup orange marmalade
2 Tbsp Grand Marnier

Notes: Make sure you are using the best marmalade you can find. When using marmalade and Grand Marnier, the temperatures for the caramel sauce and candy will not vary from the Master Formula for Caramel original guidelines. Also, depending on the variety of the jam, the orange flavor will be different, so experiment with different ones to find your favorites.

To make Sauce:

Blend the orange marmalade and Grand Marnier in a blender until completely smooth, then set aside. Prepare the Master Caramel Formula according to the sauce directions in Chapter 5. In Step 2, use only the stovetop method and add the blended orange mixture to the heavy cream, stir to combine, then allow to steep for at least 10 minutes. The goal is to get the cream hot but not boiling. The cream should be kept hot until it is used in Step 5. Return to the Master Caramel Formula and complete STEP 3 through STEP 6 For Sauce.

To make Candy:

Blend the orange marmalade and Grand Marnier in a blender until completely smooth, then set aside. Prepare the Master Caramel Formula according to the candy directions in Chapter 5. In Step 2, use only the stovetop method and add the orange mixture to the heavy cream, stir to combine, then allow to steep for at least 10 minutes. The goal is to get the cream hot but not boiling. The cream should be kept hot until it is used in Step 5. Return to the Master Caramel Formula and complete STEP 3 through STEP 11, making sure to use STEP 6 For Candy.

Chambord Caramel Sauce

1 Master Formula for Caramel
1/4 cup Chambord

Note: When using Chambord, the temperatures for the caramel sauce and candy will not vary from the Master Formula for Caramel original guidelines.

To make Sauce:

Prepare the Master Caramel Formula according to the sauce directions in Chapter 5. After completing all of STEP 5, add the Chambord and stir again to combine. Return to the Master Caramel Formula and complete STEP 6 For Sauce.

To make Candy:

Prepare the Master Caramel Formula according to the candy directions in Chapter 5. After completing all of STEP 5, add the Chambord and stir again to combine, and then return pot to medium heat and Return to the Master Caramel Formula and complete STEP 6 For Candy through STEP 11.

Rum Caramel Sauce & Candy

1 Master Formula for Caramel
1/4 cup rum (quality is important; you can try a spicy/flavored one for a more unique flavor combination)

Note: When using rum, the temperatures for the caramel sauce and candy will not vary from the Master Formula for Caramel original guidelines.

To make Sauce:

Prepare the Master Caramel Formula according to the sauce directions in Chapter 5. After completing all of STEP 5, add the rum and stir again to combine. Return to the Master Caramel Formula and complete STEP 6 For Sauce.

To make Candy:

Prepare the Master Caramel Formula according to the candy directions in Chapter 5. After completing all of STEP 5, add the rum and stir again to combine, and then return pot to medium heat and Return to the Master Caramel Formula and complete STEP 6 For Candy through STEP 11.

Strawberry Caramel Sauce & Candy

1 Master Formula for Caramel
1/2 cup seedless strawberry jam

Notes: Make sure you are using the best jam you can find, and seedless is important for maintaining a creamy texture. When using jam, the temperatures for the caramel sauce and candy will not vary from the Master Formula for Caramel original guidelines. Also, depending on the variety of the jam, the strawberry flavor will be different, so experiment with different ones to find your favorites.

To make Sauce:

Prepare the Master Caramel Formula according to the sauce directions in Chapter 5. In Step 2, use only the stovetop method and add the strawberry jam to the heavy cream, stir to combine, then allow to steep for at least 10 minutes. The goal is to get the cream hot but not boiling. The cream should be kept hot until it is used in Step 5. Return to the Master Caramel Formula and complete STEP 3 through STEP 6 For Sauce.

To make Candy:

Prepare the Master Caramel Formula according to the candy directions in Chapter 5. In Step 2, use only the stovetop method and add the strawberry jam to the heavy cream, stir to combine, then allow to steep for at least 10 minutes. The goal is to get the cream hot but not boiling. The cream should be kept hot until it is used in Step 5. Return to the Master Caramel Formula and complete STEP 3 through STEP 11, making sure to use STEP 6 For Candy.

Coffee Caramel Sauce & Candy

1 Master Formula for Caramel
1 serving instant coffee (roast and source of your choice)

Notes: Make sure you are using a high-quality instant coffee such as VIA by Starbucks. When using instant coffee, the temperatures for the caramel sauce and candy will not vary from the Master Formula for Caramel original guidelines. Also, depending on the source, roast, and blend of the instant coffee, the coffee flavor will be different, so experiment with different ones to find your favorites. I recommend that you start by using a coffee that you would like to drink as even the blonde and medium roasts produce excellent results for intensity of flavor in caramel.

To make Sauce:

Prepare the Master Caramel Formula according to the sauce directions in Chapter 5. In Step 2, use only the stovetop method and add the instant coffee to the heavy cream, stir to combine, then allow to steep for at least 10 minutes. The goal is to get the cream hot but not boiling. The cream should be kept hot until it is used in Step 5. Return to the Master Caramel Formula and complete STEP 3 through STEP 6 For Sauce.

To make Candy:

Prepare the Master Caramel Formula according to the candy directions in Chapter 5. In Step 2, use only the stovetop method and add the instant coffee to the heavy cream, stir to combine, then allow to steep for at least 10 minutes. The goal is to get the cream hot but not boiling. The cream should be kept hot until it is used in Step 5. Return to the Master Caramel Formula and complete STEP 3 through STEP 11, making sure to use STEP 6 For Candy.

Hazelnut Caramel Sauce & Candy

For Sauce Only:
1 Master Formula for Caramel
1 Tbsp **hazelnut** extract

For Candy Only:
1 Master Formula for Caramel
1 Tbsp hazelnut extract
1/2 cup finely chopped hazelnuts

Note: When using hazelnuts and hazelnut extract, the temperatures for the caramel sauce and candy will not vary from the Master Formula for Caramel original guidelines.

To make Sauce:

Prepare the Master Caramel Formula according to the sauce directions in Chapter 5. After completing all of STEP 5, add **only** the hazelnut extract and stir again to combine. Return to the Master Caramel Formula and complete STEP 6 For Sauce. (no hazelnuts are to be used in the sauce, just the extract, as otherwise the sauce would end up lumpy)

To make Candy:

Prepare the Master Caramel Formula according to the candy directions in Chapter 5. After completing all of STEP 5, add the hazelnuts **and** hazelnut extract and stir again to combine, and then return pot to medium heat and Return to the Master Caramel Formula and complete STEP 6 For Candy through STEP 11.

Maple Pecan Caramel Sauce & Candy

1 Master Formula for Caramel **with the following changes:**
STEP 3: Substitute 1 cup packed light brown sugar instead of the 1 cup of white sugar.
STEP 3: Substitute wetting the sugar with 1/2 cup real maple syrup instead of the 1/2 cup of tap water
STEP 4: Since you are making a variation that specifically uses brown sugar, then use your thermometer! Your eyes will be deceived on the caramel color due to the color of the brown sugar, so the thermometer is a key tool now.
For Candy (For Sauce is Optional): 1/2 cup chopped pecans either fine or rough chop depending upon the dessert use and personal preference.

Notes: When using these changes, the temperatures for the caramel sauce and candy will not vary from the Master Formula for Caramel original guidelines. Maple syrup varies with local and regional maple farms due to tree variety, soil composition, extraction method, collection container, processing, storage container, and if organic so experiment with options for this unique treat for the local flavor or farm of your preference.

To make Sauce:

Prepare the Master Caramel Formula according to the sauce directions in Chapter 5. In STEP 3, use the STEP 3 substitutions listed above. In STEP 4, use the thermometer to gauge your desired temperature. If desired for particular desserts, then in STEP 5, after completing all of STEP 5, add the chopped pecans and stir again to combine. Return to the Master Caramel Formula and complete STEP 6 For Sauce. In all cases, complete the caramel process through STEP 6 For Sauce.

To make Candy:

Prepare the Master Caramel Formula according to the candy directions in Chapter 5. In STEP 3 use the STEP 3 substitutions listed above. In STEP 4, use the thermometer to gauge your desired temperature. In STEP 6, use STEP 6 For Candy. At the **beginning of STEP 7**, just after you remove the pot from the heat source, add the chopped pecans, and stir again to combine. Return to the Master Caramel Formula and complete the rest of **STEP 7** through STEP 11.

Butterscotch Caramel Sauce & Candy

1 Master Formula for Caramel **with the following changes:**
STEP 3: Substitute 2 cups packed light brown sugar instead of the 2 cups of white sugar.
STEP 4: Since you are making a variation that specifically uses brown sugar, then use your thermometer! Your eyes will be deceived on the caramel color due to the color of the brown sugar, so the thermometer is a key tool now.
STEP 5: Increase the unsalted butter from 2 Tbsp to 4 Tbsp total.

Note: When using these changes, the temperatures for the caramel sauce and candy will not vary from the Master Formula for Caramel original guidelines.

To make Sauce:

Prepare the Master Caramel Formula according to the sauce directions in Chapter 5. In STEP 3, use the STEP 3 sugar substitution listed above. In STEP 4, use the thermometer to gauge your desired temperature. In STEP 5, increase the unsalted butter from the original 2 Tbsp to 4 Tbsp total. Return to the Master Caramel Formula and complete through STEP 6 For Sauce.

To make Candy:

Prepare the Master Caramel Formula according to the candy directions in Chapter 5. In STEP 3 use the STEP 3 sugar substitution listed above. In STEP 4, use the thermometer to gauge your desired temperature. In STEP 5, increase the unsalted butter from the original 2 Tbsp to 4 Tbsp total. Return to the Master Caramel Formula, In STEP 6, use STEP 6 For Candy and complete through STEP 11.

Mocha Caramel Sauce & Candy

1 Master Formula for Caramel
1 serving instant coffee (roast and source of your choice)
1/2 cup bittersweet chocolate chips

Notes: Make sure you are using a high-quality instant coffee such as VIA by Starbucks. Also, depending on the source, roast, and blend of the instant coffee, the coffee flavor will be different, so experiment with different ones to find your favorites. I recommend that you start by using a coffee that you would like to drink, as even the blonde and medium roasts produce excellent results for intensity of flavor in caramel. The temperatures will not vary from the Master Formula for Caramel original guidelines.

To make Sauce:

Prepare the Master Caramel Formula according to the sauce directions in Chapter 5. **In Step 2**, use only the stovetop method and add the instant coffee to the heavy cream, stir to combine, then allow to steep for at least 10 minutes. The goal is to get the cream hot but not boiling. The cream should be kept hot until it is used in Step 5. Return to the Master Caramel Formula and complete through STEP 5. **After completing all of STEP 5**, add the chocolate chips and stir again to combine. Return to the Master Caramel Formula and complete STEP 6 For Sauce.

To make Candy:

Prepare the Master Caramel Formula according to the candy directions in Chapter 5. **In Step 2**, use only the stovetop method and add the instant coffee to the heavy cream, stir to combine, then allow to steep for at least 10 minutes. The goal is to get the cream hot but not boiling. The cream should be kept hot until it is used in Step 5. Return to the Master Caramel Formula and complete STEP 3 through STEP 6, making sure to use STEP 6 For Candy. At the **beginning of STEP 7**, just after you remove the pot from the heat source, add the chocolate chips, and stir again to combine. Return to the Master Caramel Formula and complete the rest of **STEP 7** through STEP 11.

White Chocolate Macadamia Caramel Sauce & Candy

1 Master Formula for Caramel **with the following changes:**
1/2 cup white chocolate chips
For Candy (For Sauce is Optional): 1/2 cup macadamia nuts, roughly chopped

Notes: When using these changes, the temperatures for the caramel sauce and candy will not vary from the Master Formula for Caramel original guidelines.

To make Sauce:

Prepare the Master Caramel Formula according to the sauce directions in Chapter 5. In STEP 5, **after completing all of STEP 5**, add the white chocolate chips and stir. . If desired for particular desserts, then in STEP 5, after completing all of STEP 5 and the chocolate, add the chopped macadamia nuts and stir again to combine. Return to the Master Caramel Formula and complete STEP 6 For Sauce. In all cases, complete the caramel process through STEP 6 For Sauce.

To make Candy:

Prepare the Master Caramel Formula according to the candy directions in Chapter 5, using STEP 6 For Candy. At the **beginning of STEP 7**, just after you remove the pot from the heat source, add the white chocolate chips and macadamia nuts, and stir again to combine. Return to the Master Caramel Formula and complete the rest of **STEP 7** through STEP 11.

Oh Joy! Caramel Sauce & Candy

1 Master Formula for Caramel
1 Tbsp coconut extract (or almond extract if you prefer)
1/2 cup bittersweet chocolate chips
1/2 cup sweetened coconut flakes
For Candy (For Sauce is Optional): 1/4 cup slivered almonds

Notes: When using these changes, the temperatures for the caramel sauce and candy will not vary from the Master Formula for Caramel original guidelines.

To make Sauce:

Prepare the Master Caramel Formula according to the sauce directions in Chapter 5. In STEP 5, **after completing all of STEP 5**, add the coconut extract, chocolate, and coconut flakes and stir. If desired for particular desserts, then in STEP 5, after completing all of STEP 5, add the almonds and stir again to combine. Return to the Master Caramel Formula and complete STEP 6 For Sauce. In all cases, complete the caramel process through STEP 6 For Sauce.

To make Candy:

Prepare the Master Caramel Formula according to the candy directions in Chapter 5, using STEP 6 For Candy. At the **beginning of STEP 7**, just after you remove the pot from the heat source, add the coconut extract, chocolate, coconut flakes, and almonds and stir again to combine. Return to the Master Caramel Formula and complete the rest of **STEP 7** through STEP 11.

Turtle Sauce & Candy

1 Master Formula for Caramel
1/2 cup chocolate chips (dark or milk)
For Candy (For Sauce is Optional): 1/2 cup chopped pecans

Notes: When using these changes, the temperatures for the caramel sauce and candy will not vary from the Master Formula for Caramel original guidelines.

To make Sauce:

Prepare the Master Caramel Formula according to the sauce directions in Chapter 5. In STEP 5, **after completing all of STEP 5**, add the chocolate and stir. If desired for particular desserts, then in STEP 5, after completing all of STEP 5, add the pecans and stir again to combine. Return to the Master Caramel Formula and complete STEP 6 For Sauce. In all cases, complete the caramel process through STEP 6 For Sauce.

To make Candy:

Prepare the Master Caramel Formula according to the candy directions in Chapter 5, using STEP 6 For Candy. At the **beginning of STEP 7**, just after you remove the pot from the heat source, add the chocolate and pecans and stir again to combine. Return to the Master Caramel Formula and complete the rest of **STEP 7** through STEP 11.

Sea Salt Caramel Sauce & Candy

1 Master Formula for Caramel **with the following changes:**
STEP 5: Substitute 1/4 tsp kosher salt with 1/4 tsp of non-iodized sea salt
Sauce STEP 5 & Candy STEP 7: An additional 1 tsp of non-iodized sea salt

To make Sauce:

Prepare the Master Caramel Formula according to the sauce directions in Chapter 5. After add all ingredients of STEP 5 including the substituted salt, add the additional tsp sea salt, and stir well to combine. Return to the Master Caramel Formula and complete STEP 6 For Sauce.

To make Candy:

Prepare the Master Caramel Formula according to the candy directions in Chapter 5, including all of STEP 6 for Candy. In **STEP 7**, you pour the caramel into the glass pan, so allow that to set for 5 minutes, and then sprinkle the additional tsp sea salt on top of the caramel. Return to the Master Caramel Formula and complete the rest of **STEP 7** through STEP 11.

Apple Cinnamon Caramel Sauce & Candy

1 Master Formula for Caramel
1 tsp cinnamon
1/2 cup peeled, cored, and finely diced apple (a tart varietal is best, such as Granny Smith)

Note: When using cinnamon and apples, the temperatures for the caramel sauce and candy will not vary from the Master Formula for Caramel original guidelines. Also, depending on the varietal of the apple and the source of the cinnamon, the flavors will be different, so experiment with different ones to find your favorites.

To make Sauce:

Prepare the Master Caramel Formula according to the sauce directions in Chapter 5. **In Step 2**, use only the stovetop method and add the cinnamon to the heavy cream, then allow to steep for at least 10 minutes. The goal is to get the cream hot but not boiling. The cream should be kept hot until it is used in Step 5. If desired for particular desserts, then in STEP 5, **after completing all of STEP 5**, add the diced apples and stir again to combine. Return to the Master Caramel Formula and complete STEP 6 For Sauce. In all cases, complete the caramel process through STEP 6 For Sauce.

To make Candy:

Prepare the Master Caramel Formula according to the candy directions in Chapter 5. **In Step 2,** use only the stovetop method and add the cinnamon to the heavy cream, then allow to steep for at least 10 minutes. The goal is to get the cream hot but not boiling. The cream should be kept hot until it is used in Step 5. Return to the Master Caramel Formula and complete STEP 3 through STEP 6, using STEP 6 For Candy. At the **beginning of STEP 7**, just after you remove the pot from the heat source, add the diced apples and stir again to combine. Return to the Master Caramel Formula and complete the rest of **STEP 7** through STEP 11.

Vegan Caramel Sauce

1 Master Formula for Caramel **with the following changes:**
Substitute dairy butter with an equal amount of vegan margarine (Earth Balance is a common brand)
Substitute heavy cream with an equal amount of coconut milk or almond milk (shake well before measuring)
Omit salt (already enough in the vegan margarine)

Note: When using these vegan changes, the temperatures for the caramel sauce and candy will not vary from the Master Formula for Caramel original guidelines.

7 DESSERTS

Inside-out Caramel Apple

4 tart apples halved, seeded, cored (do not peel!)
1 tsp lemon juice diluted with 1 tsp tap water
1 Master Formula for Caramel for Candy

Note: If you want to experiment using a favorite candy from the previous recipe variations given in this guide, then feel welcome to substitute that candy variation instead of the vanilla Master Caramel Formula, as no other changes would need to be made for this inside-out recipe to work.

Using a spoon, shave out extra apple flesh until you form a bowl out the halved apple. Repeat this for the other halves. Brush the edges of the apple "bowls" with the diluted lemon juice. Place "bowl" up on a plate or tray or baking sheet. Prepare Master Formula for Caramel for candy and allow to cool for 10 minutes. Pour caramel into each apple "bowl" and allow to fully-set in the refrigerator, on the plate, uncovered for at least 15 minutes. These bowls can be kept up to a day in the refrigerator but need to be covered after the 15 minute setting time. When ready to eat, transfer fully-set caramel apple "bowls" to a cutting board, allow to set out at room temperature for 10 minutes, then slice into wedges.

For any leftover candy formula liquid, complete the Master Formula for Caramel for Candy and enjoy the bonus!

Caramel Flan

3/4 cup white granulated sugar
2 Tbsp water
4 eggs
1 1/2 cup whole milk
1 (14 oz) can sweetened condensed milk
1/2 tsp vanilla extract
1/8 tsp Kosher salt

Preheat oven to 350 F/ 176.6 C

On the stovetop, on medium heat, in a pan, cook sugar and water, stirring constantly until melted and caramel-colored.

Pour mixture into a 9-inch round baking pan, coating bottom completely. Set aside.

In a bowl, beat eggs, then whisk in milk, sweetened condensed milk, vanilla and salt. Pour this mixture over the caramelized sugar in the baking pan.

Set baking pan into a larger oven-safe pan (such as a broiler or roasting pan). Into the larger pan, pour 1-inch hot tap water. This double-pan method is referred to as a "water bath".

Place the double-pan set up into the preheated oven, on the middle rack, and bake 55 to 60 minutes or until a knife or toothpick inserted near the center comes out clean.

Once baked, remove the double-pan from the oven, remove the baking pan from the water bath, and place on a wire rack. Allow the flan to cool to room temperature. Then, transfer to the refrigerator to chill for at least 2 hours.

Remove the entire flan from the baking pan: run a knife around the edges of the pan, place a large serving platter upside down on top of the pan, flip the pan and platter over **held together**, place the two together on a countertop, and carefully raise up the baking pan straight up to remove it, leaving the flan on the platter.

Decadent Chocolate Cake with Caramel Frosting

2 cups white granulated sugar
1 3/4 cup all-purpose flour
3/4 cup cocoa powder
1 tsp Kosher salt
1 1/2 tsp baking powder
1 1/2 tsp baking soda
2 large eggs, beaten
1/2 cup canola oil (or vegetable oil)
1 cup "whole" Vit D milk
1 cup boiling water

Preheat oven to 350 F/ 176.6 C

Into 2 round, 9-inch cake pans, lightly coat with pan spray, line with parchment paper, and lightly coat with spray again.

The easiest is to use is a stand mixer with a paddle. You may use a mixer with a whisk or just a bowl and a wooden spoon or spatula as alternate methods. Combine sugar, flour, cocoa, salt, baking powder, and baking soda. Then turn on mixer to low speed and mix well. Stay on low speed, add eggs one at a time, then add oil slowly, then add milk, and allow mix to fully combine. Stay on low speed and add water, and allow to mix. The batter will look very soupy. This is normal!

Pour an equal amount of batter in each of the two pans and bake in the preheated oven on the middle rack for 15 minutes, then rotate the pans halfway and back for another 15-20 minutes for a total baking time of 30 to 35 minutes. Insert a toothpick or knife in the center of each pan; if this comes out clean on each, then these are done. If not, then bake for a few minutes more, keeping a close eye on these, then check again. When done baking, place a wire rack upside down on top of each pan, hold the rack and pan together and flip upside down, place the rack and pan onto the countertop together, and carefully raise up the baking pan straight up to remove it. Discard the parchment paper and allow the two cake rounds to cool on the wire racks for 30 minutes.

Caramel Frosting

4 sticks unsalted butter, at room temperature
1 lb confectioners' sugar (about 3 3/4 cups)
1/2 cup Dulce de Leche (see Common Formulas for recipe)
1 tsp vanilla extract
1/4 tsp non-iodized, Kosher salt

With an electric mixer, on high speed, beat the butter until fluffy, usually 3 to 5 minutes. Reduce to low speed. Slowly, in three parts, add the sugar, scraping the sides of the bowl to mix well. When the mix is creamy, add the Dulce de Leche, vanilla, and salt, then beat the mix until smooth, scraping the sides of the bowl to mix well. Apply to top of first cake round, then add second cake layer and apply to sides and top.

Crème Brulée

For Brulée:
4 cups heavy cream
2 Tbsp vanilla extract
1/2 cup white granulated sugar
6 egg yolks

Notes: The leftover egg whites can be frozen in a sealed container up to a month, then thawed for use in something else such as a meringue or biscotti.

For topping: 6 Tbsp white granulated sugar

Preheat the oven to 325 F / 162.7 C

In pot, on medium heat, add cream then simmer for 10 mins. Remove from burner and stir in vanilla extract.

In a bowl, vigorously whisk the 1/2 cup sugar and the egg yolks until it the egg yolks begin to lighten in color. Add the warm cream a little at a time, whisking continuously. (This process is called tempering the eggs, as you are raising the temperature of the eggs slowly with the warm cream being added slowly. If done too quickly, then you will just have scrambled sugary eggs.)

Divide the liquid into 6 (8 oz) ramekins. Put all ramekins on a baking or roasting pan. Pour enough hot tap water into the pan to come halfway up the sides of the ramekins.

Bake in the preheated oven, on the middle rack, just until the Brulée is mostly set but still jiggles in the center, about 40 minutes. Remove the ramekins from the pan, place on a wire rack, and cool on the countertop for 15 minutes. Then, cover each ramekin with plastic wrap film and refrigerate for at least 2 hours and up to 2-3 days.

Spread 1 Tbsp sugar evenly on top of each Brulée in the ramekin. Use a torch that is used only for food. Using that torch, make several passes to melt the sugar evenly without burning and form a crispy topping that is golden brown. Allow the Brulée to sit for at a few minutes before serving in the ramekins.

Coffee-Caramel Crème Brulée

For Brulée:
4 cups heavy whipping cream
1 Tbsp vanilla extract
2 Tbsp instant coffee
1/2 cup white granulated sugar
6 egg yolks

For topping: 6 Tbsp white granulated sugar

Note: Make sure you are using a high-quality instant coffee such as VIA by Starbucks. Also, depending on the source, roast, and blend of the instant coffee, the coffee flavor will be different, so experiment with different ones to find your favorites. I recommend that you start by using a coffee that you would like to drink, as even the blonde and medium roasts produce excellent results for intensity of flavor

Note: The leftover egg whites can be frozen in a sealed container up to a month, then thawed for use in something else such as a meringue or biscotti.

Preheat the oven to 325 F / 162.7 C

In pot, on medium heat, add cream and instant coffee then simmer for 10 mins. Remove from burner and stir in vanilla extract.

In a bowl, vigorously whisk the 1/2 cup sugar and the egg yolks until it the egg yolks begin to lighten in color. Add the warm cream a little at a time, whisking continuously. (This process is called tempering the eggs, as you are raising the temperature of the eggs slowly with the warm cream being added slowly. If done too quickly, then you will just have scrambled sugary eggs.)

Divide the liquid into 6 (8 oz) ramekins. Put all ramekins on a baking or roasting pan. Pour enough hot tap water into the pan to come halfway up the sides of the ramekins.

Bake in the preheated oven, on the middle rack, just until the Brulée is mostly set but still jiggles in the center, about 40 minutes. Remove the ramekins from the pan, place on a wire rack, and cool on the countertop for 15 minutes. Then, cover each ramekin with plastic wrap film and refrigerate for at least 2 hours and up to 2-3 days.

Spread 1 Tbsp sugar evenly on top of each Brulée in the ramekin. Use a torch that is used only for food. Using that torch, make several passes to melt the sugar evenly without burning and form a crispy topping that is golden brown. Allow the Brulée to sit for at a few minutes before serving in the ramekins.

Vanilla Caramel Cheesecake

Crust:
1 1/2 cups graham cracker crumbs
4 Tbsp white granulated sugar
1/2 stick unsalted butter, melted

Cheesecake:
3 - 8 oz packages cream cheese
1 cup white granulated sugar
1 Tbsp fresh lemon juice
2 tsp vanilla extract
1 Tbsp all-purpose flour
3 eggs, room temperature

1 cup heavy whipping cream
1 tsp vanilla extract

1/2 cup Master Caramel Formula for Sauce, cold

Topping:
1/2 cup Master Caramel Formula for Sauce, cold

Note: If you want to experiment using a favorite sauce from the previous recipe variations given in this guide, then feel welcome to substitute that sauce variation instead of the vanilla Master Caramel Formula, as no other changes would need to be made for this cheesecake recipe to work.

Note: **You will need a springform pan**. A springform has a circle bottom plate that fits into a ring and is clamped down.

Line a 10-inch springform pan with parchment paper. To do this, place just the circle bottom piece on the countertop and fit a piece of parchment paper over that circle so that all of it is covered. Then, unclamp the ring, place it over the circle bottom plate so that the parchment paper is pulled tight across the bottom plate, then clamp down the ring so that the parchment paper shows outside of the ring and can be trimmed off with scissors.

Preheat oven to 300 F / 148.8 C

In a bowl, combine graham cracker crumbs, 4 Tbsp sugar, and 1/2 stick melted unsalted butter with your hands. Mix until the consistency is mealy. Press the crust mixture into the bottom of the lined springform pan. Bake the crust for 8 minutes. Remove and place on a wire rack to cool.

Preheat oven to 325 F / 162.7

In a mixer or in a bowl with a hand mixer, blend cream cheese and remaining 1 cup sugar until fully combined and very creamy before moving forward. Add the eggs, one at a time. Add lemon juice and 2 tsp vanilla.

In separate bowl, whip with mixer or hand whisk 1 cup heavy whipping cream to stiff peak and as the cream is thickening but before it reaches stiff peak stage, add 1 tsp vanilla. Then, gently fold whipped cream into cream cheese mix, being careful not to deflate the whipped cream.

Slowly drizzle cold caramel sauce into the cream cheese mixture, and gently fold once only. Do not over mix.

Take the springform pan with the cooled crust, wrap the outside in 2 layers of aluminum foil, being careful not to tear the foil. The foil should come to the top of the pan. Place springform pan into a baking pan or roasting pan and then add hot tap water until covers at least 1 inch of the springform pan. Then, pour the cream cheese mixture into the springform pan.

Bake in the oven, on the middle rack, for 1 hour. You should begin to see small cracks in the surface of the cheesecake, and these cracks mean it is done. Turn off the heat to the oven, open the oven door, and leave the cheesecake with the "water bath" in the cooling oven for another 45 minutes. This will allow the cracks to "fill back in".

Then, remove everything from the oven, remove the springform pan from the "water bath" pan, and remove the 2 layers of foil, then let it sit uncovered on a wire rack for 30 minutes to cool in the springform pan. Then, cover the springform pan with plastic wrap film and refrigerate.

Before serving, unclamp the springform ring, carefully remove the ring (if does not separate, then run a knife around the edges and carefully try again), cut cheesecake into wedges, remove each piece from the bottom plate and parchment paper, and top each piece with the remaining caramel sauce.

Caramelized Pears in Puff Pastry

2 pears peeled, seeded, and halved (any varietal)
1/2 cup white granulated sugar
1/4 cup cool tap water
2 Tbsp unsalted butter
1 tsp lemon juice
1 tsp vanilla extract
1 sheet puff pastry
1 Tbsp melted unsalted butter
2 Tbsp white granulated sugar
4 scoops vanilla ice cream (your favorite brand and type)

Preheat oven to 350 F/ 176.6 C

Place pears flat-side down on the countertop. Drape puff pastry sheet over all four pear halves. By hand, form a shell over each one, then trim each one along the edges with a knife. Remove the shells from the pear halves and set to the side.

In a large, non-stick pan, on medium-high heat, add 1/2 cup sugar and 1/4 cup water, and heat until the sugar begins to turn a medium-amber color. Add butter, lemon juice, and vanilla extract, then stir to combine. Add pear halves with the flat-side down, and reduce heat to medium. Cook for 3 minutes.

Transfer the pear halves to a baking sheet, placing flat-side down. Leave the pan off of the burner but keep the butter mixture in the pan to use later. Cover the pear halves with the puff pastry shells. Brush the outside of the shells with the melted butter mixture from the pan and sprinkle with sugar.

In the oven, on the middle rack, bake for approximately 15 minutes, until pastry shells are golden brown. Using a heat-safe spatula, remove pear halves and place pastry side down onto plates. Drizzle butter mixture from pan over pears and add a scoop of vanilla ice cream to each plate.

Caramel Apples

4 tart apples – wash well and dry well, remove stems
1 Master Caramel Formula for Candy

Note: If you want to experiment using a favorite candy from the previous recipe variations given in this guide, then feel welcome to substitute that candy variation instead of the vanilla Master Caramel Formula, as no other changes would need to be made for this inside-out recipe to work.

Refrigerate washed and dried apples for 30 minutes. Then, insert a popsicle/craft stick into each apple from where the stem was removed, inserting the stick at least halfway into the apple but being careful not to exit the other end **and** to leave enough stick outside to grasp for eating.

Prepare Master Caramel Formula for Candy, pour into a glass bowl, allow to cool for 5 minutes, stirring occasionally.

Dip each apple in caramel candy liquid, turning slowly to coat. Place dipped apples onto wax paper.

If you plan to eat these immediately, then allow these to set out at room temperature until the caramel is set, about 5 minutes.

OR

If you are making these in advance, then place the dipped apples on a plate, tray, or baking pan lined with wax paper into the refrigerator. Once the caramel sets, then cover with plastic wrap film and leave in the refrigerator up to 3 days. When ready to eat these, place dipped apples on a countertop with the wax paper still underneath and set out, uncovered, at room temperature for 15 minutes before eating.

For any leftover candy formula liquid, complete the Master Formula for Caramel for Candy and enjoy the bonus!

Caramel Apple Pie

Crust:
1 cup all-purpose flour
1/2 tsp Kosher salt
1/4 cup Crisco
2 Tbsp unsalted butter, softened
2 1/2 Tbsp ice water (in a glass, put ice cubes into cold tap water for several minutes and portion out the measurement needed just before using)

Filling:
5 cups apples peeled, cored, and sliced (Granny Smith or other tart varietal)
1 lemon
1/2 cup Master Caramel Formula for Sauce
2 Tbsp tapioca pearls (or 4 Tbsp flour)
1 tsp cinnamon
1/2 tsp nutmeg

Topping:
1/2 cup sugar
1/2 cup all-purpose flour
1/2 cup unsalted butter

Preheat oven to 400 F / 204.4 C

Notes: The apples can be multiple varietals to offer flavor combinations. Also, the apple slices should be cut to the same thickness each time to make for even cooking.

Lastly, to find tapioca pearls in your grocery store, look in the boxed pudding mixes section for a small box or plastic bag marked as either tapioca pearls or tapioca granules.

Crust Directions:
In a bowl, add crust ingredients of flour, salt, Crisco, butter, and water, then work into dough with your hands until it begins to gluttonize (gets sticky and all ingredients are well mixed), then knead only a few more times, then try to form the mixture into a ball. If the ball does not form well, then knead a bit more and try to form the ball again. Depending upon the flour, you may need to add additional ice-cold water to make the mixture sticky enough to form the ball, but only add a little water at a time, kneading the water in before adding more. You do not want to knead any more than necessary for forming the mixture as over-mixing makes a tough crust. Once you have a dough ball, then leave that in the bowl and refrigerate for 30 minutes. Next, prepare an area to roll out your crust, such as a countertop or table, cleaning and drying the area well, then scattering a little flour on that surface a little bigger than the size your crust needs to be. Place the chilled dough ball on the floured surface and using a rolling pin, press down and roll out in different directions over and over until you have even thickness and enough surface area to fit your deep pie plate. You can do an approximate measurement by holding the plate over the dough to see if the dough is bigger than the pie plate by at least 2 inches. Once rolled out to the right size, you can fix any little tears by wetting your finger with ice water and press the dough to "seam" the rip closed. If needed, then use a little "patch" of dough to close the tear, "seaming" the patch

with your wet fingers. Gently lift one edge of your dough to fold the dough circle in half, then carefully move the entire circle of dough onto your pie plate, adjusting to cover one half and having some overlapping the plate edge, then unfold the circle to cover the entire pie plate and have some dough overlapping all of the pie plate edges. Gently press the dough so that it lies against the sides of the pie plate. Run a knife along the outer edge of the pie plate to trim off the excess dough. Place the pointer finger and thumb of one hand together with the finger pads touching each other, then place the combined fingertips at the outer edge of the plate aiming into the center and use the pointer finger of your other hand to push the edge of the dough into the point formed by the combined fingers. Move around the edge of the dough repeating this until you have "fluted" the entire circle of dough for the edge of the pie crust. Set this aside.

Filling Directions:
Discard the peel and core of the apples, then slice the apples into a large bowl. Toss the apples in the lemon juice to prevent these from browning. Add tapioca pearls, cinnamon, and nutmeg, then mix well to coat the apples. Transfer everything into the pie crust, scraping the bowl for all of the juices and granules. Move the apples around to make a hill of apples with slices spread all the way to the edges, keeping in mind that the apples will reduce in size when baking and to not be concerned if the mound appears tall right now. Then, drizzle 1/2 cup of the Master Caramel Formula for Sauce over the apple filling.

Topping Directions:
In a bowl, add flour and sugar then mix. Add soft butter and with your hands, knead and blend into a sticky consistency of wet sand. Using your fingers, pinch small amounts (about the size of a marble or penny) and drop those randomly on top of the apple filling, allowing overlapping , and using all of the mixture. The dropped pieces will spread out during baking and make a textured topping that covers most or all of the pie. Dropping the topping "globs" is a fun step for kids to help with!

Baking Directions:
Note: On the lower rack, place either a large baking pan/sheet or a large piece of aluminum foil to cover the rack, as this will catch the drips and spills of the pie. This makes for a much easier clean up and prevents oven fires.

In the oven, on the middle rack, in the center, bake for 10 minutes at 400 F / 204.4 C. Then reduce the heat to 375 F / 190.5 C and bake for an additional 45 - 50 minutes. Then check the pie first by piercing one of the top apple slices with a fork to see if it pierces easily; second, the topping should be a golden brown. If not done, then continue to bake at 375 F / 190.5 C, checking every 10 minutes for doneness. Then, remove from the oven and transfer to a wire rack to cool for 30 minutes before eating. Once completely cool, the pie plate can be covered with plastic wrap film and refrigerated up to a week. The aluminum foil for "drips" should be discarded as foil cannot be used to cover pie.

Caramel Bars

1 cup all-purpose flour
1 cup rolled oats
3/4 cup brown sugar
1/2 tsp baking soda
1/4 tsp Kosher salt
3/4 cup unsalted butter, melted
1/2 cup semisweet chocolate chips
1/2 cup chopped walnuts
2 cups Master Caramel Formula for Candy, however only cook to 238 F / 114.4 C

Note: If you want to experiment using a favorite candy from the previous recipe variations given in this guide, then feel welcome to substitute that candy variation instead of the vanilla Master Caramel Formula, as no other changes, other than the same 238 F / 114.4 C temperature as noted above, would need to be made for this caramel bars recipe to work.

Preheat oven to 350 F/ 176.6 C

Lightly coat any 9x13 inch baking pan with nonstick cooking spray.

In a bowl, add flour, oats, brown sugar, baking soda and salt, then mix. Add in the melted butter and mix well. Press half of the mixture into the bottom of the baking pan. Set aside the other half of the mixture.

In the oven, on the middle rack, in the center, bake the crust for 7 minutes. Remove and place on a wire rack. Being careful with the hot pan, sprinkle in chocolate chips and walnuts. Pour the prepared, hot caramel candy in next, then scatter crumbles of the remaining crust mixture over everything.

Return the baking pan to the oven and bake for an additional 12 to 15 minutes, or until the top is lightly toasted. Remove and place on a wire rack. Cut while it is still warm, but allow it to come to room temperature before serving. Once at room temperature, may be covered with a matching plastic lid or plastic wrap film or aluminum foil and then refrigerated for up to a week.

Caramel Pecan Tart

3 1/2 cups pecans
2 cups all-purpose flour
2/3 cup powdered sugar
3/4 cup unsalted butter, cubed
1 Master Formula for Caramel for Sauce

Note: **You will need an 11-inch tart pan for this recipe.** A tart pan is metal and has angled, fluted (wavy) sides with a bottom lip and a removable circle plate on the bottom that sits on the lip. Lightly coat the tart pan with nonstick spray before use.

If you do not have a tart pan, then you may use a springform pan as described in the cheesecake recipe. Just as with the cheesecake, you must line the springform circle plate with parchment paper when using it for a tart.

Preheat oven to 350 F/ 176.6 C

Place pecans on a baking sheet. In the oven, on middle rack, bake for about 6 minutes or until lightly toasted. Remove from baking sheet to a tray or pan and spread to single layer to cool. Set aside.

Lightly coat the bottom and sides of the tart pan with nonstick cooking spray.

In a bowl, mix flour and powdered sugar, add butter and mix together with hands until mixture is well combined. Press mixture to form an even layer of crust on the bottom and up sides of the tart pan to the top.

In the oven, on the middle rack, bake the crust 15 to 20 minutes or until edges are lightly browned. Remove and place on a wire rack at least 30 minutes, until completely cooled.

Prepare the Master Formula for Caramel for sauce and let cool in a glass bowl for 10 minutes, then stir in pecans to caramel sauce. Pour the caramel sauce mixture into the cooled tart crust. In the oven, on the middle rack, bake the tart for 15 to 20 minutes until golden and bubbly. Remove the tart pan and place on a wire rack at least 45 minutes, until completely cool.

To remove the tart from the tart pan, gently but firmly push up (from underneath) on the circle bottom plate to release the base plate from the fluted ring. Set out a serving plate or tray, then using a thin spatula, gently nudge the tart, while holding it at an angle, until it slides onto the serving plate / tray.

To remove the tart from a springform pan, place the pan on a countertop, run a knife around the inside edge to ensure separation of the crust from the ring, then unclamp the ring, gently remove the ring straight up, set out a serving plate of tray, grasp edge of parchment paper and keeping the paper under the tart, pull the tart off of the metal plate and onto the serving plate. The paper will need to stay under the tart, so when cutting the pieces, try to not cut the parchment paper, then use a thin spatula to separate the piece off of the paper before putting on a plate.

The tart may be covered with plastic wrap film and refrigerated for up to a week. You may serve tart pieces immediately after removing from the refrigerator.

Caramel Banana Pudding

4 cups "day old" French or sourdough bread in 1-inch pieces
1/4 cup unsalted butter, melted
3 eggs
2 cups "whole" Vitamin D milk
1/2 cup white granulated sugar
2 tsp vanilla extract
1/2 tsp ground cinnamon
1/2 tsp ground nutmeg
1/2 tsp Kosher salt
1 1/2 cups firm bananas sliced into 1/4-inch thick circles
1 Master Formula for Caramel for Sauce, warm

Preheat oven to 375 F / 190.5 C

Lightly coat a 2 quart glass, ceramic, or metal pan with nonstick spray.

Place cubed bread in a large bowl.

In another bowl, beat eggs, then add milk, sugar, butter, vanilla, cinnamon, nutmeg, and salt. Then, stir in bananas. Pour this mixture over the bread cubes and stir bread to coat.

Transfer everything to the greased pan and put in the preheated oven on the middle rack. Bake, uncovered, for 30 to 40 minutes or until a knife or toothpick inserted near the center comes out clean. For each portion of bread pudding, spoon or pour warmed up caramel sauce over the top.

ABOUT THE AUTHOR

James Shipley is a Chef and Chocolatier with a passion for international cuisine and for his Native American roots. Chef James is influenced by his grandmother Genevieve, a lifelong chef in the logging heydays of the Minnesota Northwoods. Chef James' personal philosophy of food is to let the ingredients speak, so he designs recipes which highlight the natural greatness in each item.

Chef James' custom chocolate truffles and other handcrafted treats can be purchased at www.TwoBearsChocolates.com

Chef James' other cookbooks as well as fiction and non-fiction books can be purchased through links at www.ShipleyPublishing.com

Other current James Shipley titles:
24-Day Challenge Cookbook
The Ahimsa Cookbook
The Artisans Cafe Cookbook
Chocolate Truffles: A Beginner's Guide
Inspiration to Run
The Bear Mindset for Success
Zombie Apocalypse Manual

Upcoming James Shipley titles to look for in 2013:
The Next 30 Days Cookbook
Bread: A Beginner's Guide

Made in the USA
San Bernardino, CA
05 November 2013